Copyright © 2003 by The University of British Columbia

2003 2004 2005 2006 2007   5 4 3 2 1

All rights to this work are reserved. No portion of this work may be reproduced, stored in a digital retrieval system or transmitted in any form or by any means without the express written permission of The University of British Columbia, or, in the case of photocopying or other reprography, a license from the Canadian Copyright Licensing Agency.

The University of British Columbia
2329 West Mall
Vancouver, BC, Canada
V6T 1Z4

National Library of Canada Cataloguing in Publication Data

Skene, Wayne, 1941-
  UBC : a portrait / Wayne Skene

  ISBN 0-9732584-0-3 (bound).—ISBN 0-9732584-1-1 (pbk.)

  1. University of British Columbia. I. University of British Columbia. II. Title.
LE3.B82S53 2003   378.711'33   C2003-910370-6

This book was produced for The University of British Columbia by:

Tribute Books Inc.
12777-18th Avenue
Surrey, British Columbia
V4A 1W2
www.tributebooks.ca

Design by Chris Dahl
Editing by Brian Scrivener
All photographs copyright The University of British Columbia, unless otherwise noted.
Printed and bound in Canada by Friesens

ACKNOWLEDGMENTS

Tribute Books would like to thank Dr. Herbert Rosengarten, Executive Director, UBC President's Office, for envisioning this book and helping us bring it to life under his sensitive direction. We would also like to acknowledge the contribution of University Archivist Chris Hives, whose efficiency and dedication to keeping UBC's past alive assisted us greatly. Thanks, too, to Sid Katz, Executive Director, Office of Community Affairs, for beating the UBC research drum so loudly and persistently. Innumerable other people at the University met with us to discuss this project in its early stages and helped shape its content and design; we are grateful to them all. The people of UBC Public Affairs were accommodating and helpful. And Andrea Lam was a tireless photographic researcher. UBC Reports and *Trek* Magazine proved to be valuable sources of information.

The following photographers and photographic studios contributed to these pages: Dolores Baswick, Roger Brooks, John Chong, Michelle Cook, Chris Dahl (pages 110-11, ©), Perry Danforth, Martin Dee/UBC Telestudios, Janis Franklin, Paul Joseph, Kairos Unlimited, Kent Kallberg, Bill Keay /Vancouver Sun (page 49, bottom, ©), Richard Lam, Chloe Lewis (page 49, top, ©), Dianne Longson (pages 12, 80-81, 85 ©) Bill McLennan, Elizabeth Minish (page 69, bottom, ©), Greg Morton, Chris Petty (page 108, ©), Telestudios, Peter Timmermans (pages 59, top, 63, 119-122, ©), Jonathan Vaughan, Alex Waterhouse-Hayward (page 84, top, ©), June West (pages 82-83, 84, bottom, ©).

We are grateful to the following organizations and institutions that contributed photographs and other assistance: Cecil Green Park House, The Chan Centre for the Performing Arts, Frederic Wood Theatre, Green College, The Morris and Helen Belkin Gallery, The Museum of Anthropology, St. John's College, The Media Group, TRIUMF, UBC Alumni Association, UBC Archives, UBC Ceremonies and Events, UBC Enrolment Services, UBC Forestry, UBC Library, UBC Media Services, UBC Music Faculty, UBC Sports Hall of Fame, UBC Public Affairs.

UBC – A PORTRAIT

BY WAYNE SKENE

Education is for the preservation
and development of the tribe.
And the tribe is now the human race.
          – EARLE BIRNEY, 1966

Teacher, poet, intellectual anarchist and one of Canada's finest
writers, Earle Birney left an indelible mark on UBC. A UBC
alumnus, he returned to campus in 1946 to teach English on the
condition he could teach at least one course in creative writing—
"the first stone in a little shelter for the creative student naked in
academia." Birney's initiative led to the establishment of UBC's
Department of Creative Writing, the first of its kind in the country.

A PLACE THAT INSPIRES

THERE IS NO OTHER PLACE on earth where nature and learning merge more dramatically and more spectacularly than at the main campus site of the University of British Columbia. UBC is an international centre of advanced research and learning which occupies one of the most beautiful settings in the world. Lying on the western edge of Vancouver's Point Grey peninsula, it is rimmed on the west, south and north by the Georgia Strait and Burrard Inlet waters, backed in the east by the lush forests of the Pacific Spirit Regional Park and, in the distance, provided with vistas of the Coast Mountain range and the wilderness encompassing Howe Sound.

UBC's campus inspires and rewards those who come prepared to study rigorously, learn in a scholarly environment and acquire new knowledge for an adventurous future.

UBC and its luxuriant scenery can transfix visitors and overwhelm newly arrived students. It is a place that attracts the best-and-the-brightest, triggering in them strong feelings of confidence and belonging. And it draws much of its energy from the city of Vancouver, that urban jewel situated to the east of the university lands, a city considered to be one of the most attractive and liveable on the planet. It is a centre rich with life's choices: a varied array of cultural institutions, personal recreation alternatives, professional sports and a dynamic entertainment, commercial and business core.

The combined energies of Vancouver and the University of British Columbia create a place unlike any other, a place that inspires.

UBC students begin their "Pilgrimage" protest—or "Great Trek"—
in downtown Vancouver, with no small amount of public interest or support.

UBC's first home—the "Fairview shacks"—overflowed. In 1921/22, 1,200 students
squeezed into accommodation for fewer than 400. Professors held classes in private
homes, church basements and Sunday Schools. One chemistry class was held in a tent.

BEGINNINGS

CAMBRIDGE ON THE PACIFIC

IN THE SUMMER OF 1914, a year after accepting the role of first President of the University of British Columbia, and a year before classes would begin, Dr. Frank F. Wesbrook chose a motto for UBC he hoped would inspire students and faculty for years to come.

He had narrowed the choice down to *Carpe diem* (translated then as "Improve the Day") or *Tuum est* ("It is Yours"). He opted for *Tuum est*. It was a perceptive choice, for two reasons: First, Wesbrook believed strongly that an educational institution should serve the needs and aspirations of all the people of the province. UBC would be "theirs" in the universal sense. Second, given the challenges UBC students would eventually face, the strength of character they would display, and the initiatives they would undertake to see "their" university grow and prosper, *Tuum est* made for a prophetically fitting motto.

"A country comes of age when it moves beyond geography into history".

—GEORGE WOODCOCK *joined UBC's English department in 1956. In 1959 he founded* Canadian Literature, *the first periodical devoted entirely to Canadian writing. During his career, Woodcock wrote and edited more than 120 titles, ranging from biography and history to travel and poetry.*

UBC students laid claim to the unfinished campus by forming a mammoth "UBC" on the muddy, barren ground.

UBC's first President, Dr. Frank Wesbrook, toiled valiantly to see his dream of a "second Cambridge on the Pacific" materialize.

THE PROVINCE of British Columbia that entered Confederation in 1871 was a rough-hewn territory, with a small population of about 10,000 whites and 25,000 aboriginals spread over a vast, mountainous area, rich with natural resources but prone to rocky and lengthy swings of boom-and-bust economic cycles. Still, as rugged and as tenuous as things were, six years after B.C. joined Canada, Superintendent of Education John Jessop proposed the building of a provincial university. In 1890 "An Act Respecting the University of British Columbia" was passed by the provincial legislature, but political rivalry between Vancouver Island and the mainland over where the university would eventually be situated made for a shaky foundation upon which to build UBC. The first meeting in 1891 of the new university's senate failed to raise a quorum and the Act was allowed to lapse. To fill the growing gap in the province's needs for higher education, Vancouver's School Board established Vancouver College in 1899 and sought affiliation with McGill University in Montreal. After seven years, McGill University took over Vancouver College and renamed it "McGill University College of British Columbia." Unfortunately, MUCBC offered only two-year programs in arts and sciences, requiring students to complete their degrees out-of-province.

A new Minister of Education, Henry Esson Young, accepted his post with the proviso he would be free to establish a B.C.-based university. A "University Endowment Act" was passed in 1907. It provided for the funding of a university through the sale of two million acres of Crown land in central and northern B.C. The province reneged on the financing offer, having spent the money on risky railway ventures. In 1908 the legislature passed a second University Act, declaring the intended university to be non-sectarian, co-educational and tuition-free to qualified students. Undaunted by events and unkept promises, Young ploughed ahead and in 1910 guided the decision to choose Point Grey as the site for the new university. He held an architectural competition and, in 1913, selected Dr. Frank Wesbrook, Dean of Medicine at the University of Minnesota and a University of Manitoba graduate, as UBC's first president.

Wesbrook began where Young left off. With infectious enthusiasm for building what he referred to as his "Cambridge on the Pacific," he supervised the clearing of 150 acres of Point Grey land, began the selection of faculty and staff, saw the steel skeleton of the Science building erected on site and commissioned an old friend and colleague, the University of Minnesota's librarian J.T. Gerould, to travel, in the summer of 1914, to Europe and purchase books for the all-important UBC Library.

The University opened on September 30, 1915—but not in its intended location. World War I had extinguished plans for the opening of UBC at Point Grey. Provincial funding was reduced to a trickle. Building and classroom construction at Point Grey came to a halt, forcing the University to take over the temporary wooden buildings that the now disbanded MUCBC had used at the Vancouver General Hospital's Fairview properties. It would be another decade before the cramped and shabby four "Fairview shacks" were replaced. For that memorable decade, UBC students persevered in the Fairview facilities, talking in droll terms about the inadequacies, like having a "library" consisting of a couple of rooms in the tuberculosis block, and where a "full house" meant all chairs were taken while dozens of students were forced to study while standing.

THE
GATES

"He who enters a university walks on hallowed ground."
—JAMES BRYANT CONANT, PRESIDENT,
HARVARD UNIVERSITY, 1933 TO 1953

THE STUDENTS HAD NO RESIDENCES, nor was there a hall large enough in which all the first 379 undergraduates and 34 faculty members could gather.

Despite the struggle and the continuing challenges, the new university got under way, fuelled by enthusiasm and an optimistic vision of the future. An Alma Mater Society was formed, and in December 1916 the first undergraduate newspaper was published under the title of *Anonymous*, which then became the *UbiCee* and finally the *Ubyssey*, apparently in an attempt to draw parallels between the students' struggles and Odysseus' perilous journeys. *Ubyssey* went on to become one of the most outspoken and respected student publications in the country, spawning such journalistic luminaries as author and Order of Canada recipient Pierre Berton, columnist and author Allan Fotheringham, and humorist Eric Nicol.

By the early 1920s there was still no sign the provincial government was prepared to alleviate the situation by resuming construction at Point Grey. But a strange phenomenon began to grow. The close quarters, the maturity of the returned veterans, their willingness to question authority—constructively, rather than destructively—and that visceral sense of ownership in "their" university, produced an increasingly united student body, helped along by a sense of common purpose with faculty members. In 1922, frustrated and unwilling to take it any longer, the students began a province-wide "Build the University" campaign, organized to persuade the provincial government to finish construction of the Point Grey campus. A petition was circulated around the province and students went door-to-door amassing signatures. Finally, 56,000 signatures were gathered, packed into seven suitcases and presented to the Speaker of the Legislature in Victoria.

UBC's first "Trekkers" (above) take possession of their unfinished Science building in what might have been Canada's first "sit in."

The cover (left) of UBC's 1917 annual graduating class publication, later known as the Totem.

But the big event, one that truly caught the attention of politicians and the general public alike, took place on Saturday, October 28, 1922, when close to 1,200 UBC students held a "Pilgrimage" (later called the "Great Trek"), marching, complete with placards, banners, floats and a band, from downtown Vancouver to the remote Point Grey site while chanting:

> *We're through with tents and hovels,*
> *We're done with shingle stain,*
> *That's why we want you to join us*
> *And carry our Campaign.*
> *The government can't refuse us,*
> *No matter what they say,*
> *For we'll get the people voting*
> *For our new home at Point Grey.*

Arriving at Point Grey, filled with the tingle of camaraderie, the students proceeded to occupy the weathered, eight-year-old skeleton of the Science building. The Great Trek ended with the students' dedication of a cairn of stones symbolizing a structure around which a finished university would soon be built. The students' persistence, backed by strong public support, convinced the provincial government to resume work at Point Grey. Construction got under way again, and on September 22, 1925, 1,400 students crowded into the newly constructed auditorium and stood for the University's inaugural general assembly.

The UBC students of the 1920s were an unusual generation; a resolute breed whose delight in their emancipation and the full potential of their new campus was unaffected by the dust, litter and piles of debris. The entire Trek enterprise would be the beginning of a statement of student ownership that would help define the University as it grew and strengthened, a trend that endures among UBC students to this very day. When times got tough, and the need was clearly there, it would be students who would most eagerly respond to the call: whether that was taking responsibility for the construction of a new gymnasium in 1929; blocking the provincial government's efforts during the Great Depression to close their university; covering the cost of building Brock Hall in 1940, the Armoury in 1941, the War Memorial Gymnasium in 1951, the Student Union Building in 1968; or overcoming the innumerable challenges UBC would face as it transformed itself over the decades into one of the world's preeminent universities. It was, after all, "their" university.

On September 22, 1925, 1,400 students crowded into their newly constructed auditorium (above) for the University's first annual general assembly.

UBC's first classes were barely under way in 1915 when students eagerly organized a men's ice hockey team and a women's field hockey team.

The University of British Columbia: There is no other place on earth where nature and learning merge so dramatically and so spectacularly.

PEOPLE

A UNIVERSITY PRESIDENT functions much like the mayor of a good-sized city. UBC's annual budget is roughly one billion dollars. Each day, as many as 37,000 "citizens" arrive for classes and assignments. To see to their scholarly needs and creature comforts, the University relies on more than 9,000 full-time employees (3,500 professors, researchers and associates, 1,700 managers and 4,200 support staff) and 5,000 part-time workers.

The "mayor's" job isn't one that just calls for ministering to the needs of students and academics. It requires many of the same talents an elected chief magistrate would be called upon to exhibit in office. With the help of "council" (the Board of Governors, the Senate, university vice-presidents and others) the mayor's responsibilities can range from setting housing policy to solving traffic problems, from initiating long-term, multi-million-dollar capital plans to helping set the goal for the annual United Way campaign.

But like running a city, the job cannot be carried out by one person. To be successful—to ensure UBC grows, meets the needs of its community, makes possible a progressive future—the president must be supported by purposeful, committed people, dedicated to making "their University" the best that it can be.

Since Martha Piper—UBC's 11th President—arrived at UBC in 1997 she has instilled the institution with new energy and vision. With the help of faculty, staff and students, she provided guidance for the University's Trek 2000 strategy for the future.

GREATNESS comes in many shapes, sizes and propensities. On October 13, 1993, Dr. Michael Smith, a soft-spoken, much-respected biotechnology professor at the UBC's Faculty of Medicine, was awarded a Nobel Prize in chemistry for discovering site-directed mutagenesis—the ability to make a genetic mutation precisely at any spot in a DNA molecule. It was one of the most significant scientific advances of the century and one that made Michael Smith a legend. In Smith's case he added a degree of generosity to his new-found fame by giving his Nobel Prize money—half-a-million dollars—to other scientific organizations in need of funding. His motivation was to help more people understand science and technology. Dr. Smith's discovery was, to a great extent, the birth of the biotechnology revolution. It holds enormous implications for mankind—in the form of new medicines, more productive agriculture methods and more efficient industrial techniques and processes.

Michael Smith, who died of cancer on October 4, 2000, was a natural leader. His reputation and accomplishments have helped attract to UBC some of the most talented researchers in his field. One of his most notable protégés is

RESEARCH EXCELLENCE

Dr. Brett Finlay, a professor of Biochemistry and Molecular Biology and Immunology recruited by Smith in 1989. Brett Finlay's research in UBC's Biotechnology Laboratory focuses on the interactions between disease-causing bacteria and their host cells. In 1997, Finlay and his research team discovered that *E.coli* bacteria insert a protein into healthy host cells to create receptive landing areas for the bacteria. This led to the ground-breaking development of a cattle vaccine that prevents growth of *E.coli*—a treatment that could save millions of lives. For this remarkable research accomplishment, Finlay received one of UBC's most prestigious academic honours, an honour last held by the late Michael Smith: he was named the Peter Wall Institute Distinguished Professor.

Michael Smith's awards, in addition to his Nobel Prize, included Companion of the Order of Canada, Fellow, Royal Society of Canada and Fellow, Royal Society of London.

In 2002, Canadian Living *magazine named Brett Finlay (opposite) one of the 10 Canadian scientists most likely to save your life.*

CREATING NEW KNOWLEDGE

Indira Samarasekera (above) was appointed UBC's Vice-President, Research in May 2000. Dr. Samarasekera is the former Director of the Centre for Metallurgical Process Engineering in the Department of Metals and Materials Engineering at UBC.

"Creative, collaborative effort and the continual looking outwards beyond the known: these integral elements of UBC's history are also the hallmarks of its many researchers, whose brilliance has made UBC one of Canada's leading research universities."

—INDIRA SAMARASEKERA, VICE-PRESIDENT, RESEARCH; OFFICER OF THE ORDER OF CANADA

THE UNIVERSITY is one of the most dynamic institutions in our society. It stands at the forefront of human knowledge and understanding, serving as a respected foundation for debate, discovery and enlightenment, providing answers and solutions for some of society's most pressing issues.

The University of British Columbia is one of Canada's most important social institutions, one of the three most significant research and teaching facilities in the country. It provides an intellectually vigorous environment that values academic freedom, creativity and scholarly integrity in the creation of new knowledge. Its reputation is growing on both national and international fronts. By strengthening its research and scholarly capabilities, by creating a first-class learning environment and by developing opportunities to reach out to the community at large, UBC will continue to build a university that wins high praise at home and abroad as a significant player on the international university scene.

World-renowned geneticist Dr. Michael Hayden (left) is on the path to finding a cure for some of life's most crippling diseases. Hayden's work investigates the relationship between genes and disease. His studies have focused on two areas: a predictive test for Huntington's Disease and identifying new genes associated with high density lipoprotein, or "good" cholesterol. Hayden's work could lead to a drug mitigating heart disease. He has also established the only national program in the world that seeks to determine the psychological effects of genetic testing on patients.

It began in November 1998, following a year-long consultation with the people of UBC and the wider community. The University published a dynamic document that would guide it into the new millennium. *Trek 2000: A Vision for the 21st Century*, articulates the University's mission and provides a framework for action over a five-to-ten-year period. Its goal? To help UBC become the best university in Canada.

The goal of *Trek 2000* is to provide UBC students, faculty and staff with the best possible resources and conditions for learning and research and create a working environment dedicated to excellence. UBC will strive to create new knowledge, prepare its students for fulfilling careers and improve the quality of life through leading-edge research. UBC graduates will possess excellent research and communication skills, be knowledgeable, flexible and innovative, and will recognize the importance of understanding societies other than their own.

Trek 2000: A Vision for the 21st Century rests upon five important pillars:

1. **People** ... are UBC's greatest resource. People make universities great and great universities have always provided an intellectually stimulating environment for people to come together, share ideas and broaden human understanding. The *Trek 2000* mission is to ensure that UBC attracts and supports the very best.

2. **Learning** ... is at the core of the academic experience. UBC is focused on providing students with an intellectually challenging education that takes advantage of its unique social and cultural make-up, geographical location and research environment.

3. **Research** ... UBC encourages original research to increase knowledge and understanding for the benefit of society and to improve the quality of our lives.

4. **Community** ... UBC will collaborate with its local and regional communities to foster intellectual, social, cultural and economic development in the region, the province and across the country.

5. **Internationalization** ... UBC will participate as an active member of the society of the 21st century by educating future citizens to think globally.

A "NEW" MILLENNIUM

Robert Hancock (opposite), Officer of the Order of Canada, Microbiologist and Immunologist, studies "superbugs" and the role antibiotics play in their evolution. Hancock is developing new ways to combat these bugs using very small proteins called peptides. His research may lead to treatments for multi-resistant staph, tuberculosis and even cystic fibrosis.

RESEARCH AT THE EDGE OF THE UNIVERSE

In a heavily wooded forest that envelops the southerly extreme of the UBC campus there sits an orderly but hardly imposing series of buildings within which nature's basic secrets are being probed, tested and challenged. TRIUMF is the home of the world's largest cyclotron. It is a world of atoms, neutrons, quarks, leptons and short-lived particles called "pions," all leading us to a greater understanding of the properties of matter and subatomic particles—currently one of the most exciting frontiers of human knowledge.

Joanna Staniszkis (above) is a textile artist in the Agricultural Sciences faculty who turned seeds forgotten in her pocket into the Linen Project, an artistic exploration of the fabric-making process.

INNOVATION IN LEARNING

TEACHING AND RESEARCH are inextricably linked at UBC. Researchers are expected to use their research as tools in their teaching, and teachers transfer the learning that occurs in the classroom to their research laboratories. It makes for an outstanding learning environment. The synergy created produces a dynamic, evolving university attuned to innovation and change.

UBC's inventive Science One, Coordinated Sciences program and the Integrated Science Program are interdisciplinary enterprises that have helped change the way students learn. A nationally recognized 3M Teaching Fellow and Killam Teaching Prize recipient, Dr. Lee Gass, was instrumental in establishing all three programs.

Science One, for instance, places 24 students in a class with four professors from disparate disciplines and exposes them to a broader understanding of various subjects. "For example, with assistance from a chemist, a physicist and a mathematician, a biologist can teach students about photosynthesis at a much deeper level," Lee Gass explains. "When students embrace this kind of learning, it can be life-changing."

The groundwork for Science One was laid by the Arts One program. Since 1967 Arts One has brought students together in small groups in which they discover how literature, philosophy, history and politics influence one another.

Lee Gass (above) was named Canadian Professor of the Year for 2002 by the Council for Advancement and Support of Education. Dr. Gass was unanimously chosen from among 16 nominees from Canadian universities. The award recognizes his dedication to undergraduate teaching and service to industry, community and the teaching profession.

UBC'S REPUTATION as a first-class research institution has grown dramatically over the past few years. The availability of funding and the quality of the research conducted at UBC attract some of the most accomplished researchers and teachers in the country—and from other countries as well.

UBC attracts more funding, both public and private, than any other university in Western Canada. It frequently ranks first in grants received from the Social Sciences and Humanities Research Council and the Canada Council and is one of the top two university recipients of Medical/Science grants. UBC researchers conduct more than 4,000 research projects annually and UBC ranks among the top ten universities in North America for the number of spin-off companies created. In fiscal year 2001/02, UBC acquired roughly $260 million in research funding from all sources—a 30-percent increase over the previous year. The Canada Research Chair program—created by the federal government to stem Canada's "brain drain" and draw top researchers from abroad—has allocated $120 million for 156 UBC Chairs over a five-year period. By the end of 2002, the Canadian Foundation for Innovation had allocated $154 million for 169 UBC projects—the largest amount awarded to any university in Canada. Currently, more than 160 UBC faculty members—about one in 10—belong to the Royal Society of Canada, an honour bestowed only on researchers whose work has had a profound impact on the Sciences and Humanities in Canada.

PEOPLE MAKE UNIVERSITIES GREAT

Izak Benbasat, Professor, Commerce and Business Administration, Canada Research Chair, is working on the electronic retail environment and the comparative lack of human contact during transactions. His work will help guide e-business in how to foster a strong electronic customer base and should improve customer service for electronic shoppers: "UBC has regularly been the number one business school in Canada for research accomplishments and is recognized as such internationally."

In 2002, English professor William New (opposite) was named University Killam Professor, the highest honour bestowed by UBC on its faculty. He is a prolific author with 40 books to his credit as well as being the editor of the Encyclopedia of Literature in Canada, *a copy of which was presented to Her Majesty Queen Elizabeth on her visit to UBC in October 2002. "One of the exciting things about teaching is the contact with the students. The fact that young people are continually learning and discovering things means that they are teaching you as you are teaching them."*

Andrew Dawes (left), a School of Music professor, is the founder of Canada's internationally recognized Orford String Quartet, the recipient of numerous Juno Awards, an Officer of the Order of Canada and the recipient of the Dorothy Somerset Award for Performance and Development in the Visual and Performing Arts. Dawes is still struck by the enormous talent that seems wrapped in each new student: "Some kids are just amazing. They are almost ahead of you. It is hard to keep up."

UBC geneticist and Canada Research Chair holder Elizabeth Simpson (opposite) thinks some brain disorders and mental illnesses are linked to mutated genes. She studies mice because their genetic and chemical make-up, and their social structures, are similar to ours: "There is a growing field recognizing the potential of mice to study human brain disorders. Even in a mouse, it's quite a surprise that a single gene would do this and be able to change the brain that much."

Associate Professor Kishor Wasan (right), awarded a Killam Teaching Prize, and director of the Faculty of Pharmaceutical Science's undergraduate Pharmaceutical Sciences Summer Student Research Program: "We don't just train pharmacists here. We train pharmaceutical scientists."

Robert Evans (right), is a Fellow of The Royal Society of Canada and an eminent health-care economist at UBC. "My research is showing that we are in a health-care crisis, but not the one people may think. The 'crisis' is in public confidence and understanding, not in financial sustainability."

Janet Werker (below right) is a Professor of Psychology who studies normal infant language development: "I have the hope that within my lifetime some of the kinds of discoveries I've contributed to will be used to help infants and children who are not developing properly."

UBC: BUILDING A GLOBAL PERSPECTIVE

WE LIVE IN AN ERA of unprecedented global interdependence. International terrorism and rogue military threats dangerously erode protective multilateral alliances. Environmental concerns—pollution, overpopulation, resource depletion—transcend national boundaries and require cooperative solutions. Religious conflicts and ethnic confrontations call for greater enforcement of international law to protect human rights. New communication technology and increasing global trade are re-shaping world economies. These new forces of change demand a broader and deeper understanding of foreign cultures and international issues. International exchange is now a vital mechanism for maintaining intercultural relationships.

One of a university's key roles in society is contributing to the discussion of issues that impact society as a whole. UBC's Liu Institute for Global Issues brings together faculty, distinguished visitors, students, government officials, members of the business community and public organizations from around the world to examine and debate urgent global issues. The Liu Institute is founded on the principle that scholars and practitioners, working together, have the capacity to produce inventive solutions of value to governments. Acting as an ambassador for global public policy issues is a unique role for UBC to play, and one that strongly enhances its reputation as an academic pioneer in international exchange.

Formerly Canada's Minister of External Affairs, Lloyd Axworthy (right) is Director and CEO of the Liu Institute: "We must play a role in resolving global issues. In our interconnected world our own security is indivisible from our neighbour's. The basic rights of people are fundamental to world stability."

Well-known Canadian pollster Angus Reid (opposite), former founder, chairman and CEO of the Angus Reid Group, joined the Liu Institute as a senior fellow and adjunct professor in 2002.

THE UNDERGRADUATE EXPERIENCE

WORLD-RENOWNED faculty, challenging academic programs, leading-edge facilities for learning and exciting social and athletic activities—all contribute to making UBC an unparalleled experience for students. But what really distinguishes UBC is the quality of the students it draws. UBC is committed to becoming Canada's best university, and within that quest, it must attract talented students and help prepare them to meet life's challenges. The character and diversity of its undergraduate students make for a lively intellectual environment, one that fosters creativity and innovation. Each year the quality of UBC's student body increases, the bar to admission always edging upwards. But the cost of that education should not be a barrier to qualified applicants. UBC is committed to a policy that states no domestic student, otherwise qualified, will be excluded from attending the University for financial reasons alone.

UBC is focused on providing students with an intellectually challenging education that takes advantage of its unique social and cultural make-up, unmatched geographical location and top-class research environment. At UBC, students have the opportunity to work with peers and professors, to engage in original research and innovative learning approaches that link the classroom with the real world. Arts One, Science One and the Foundations programs challenge and encourage new students to transcend traditional boundaries between disciplines.

IMAGINE UBC

For many first-year university students—straight out of the tight, homey familiarity of high school—the first day on campus can be a raucous, apprehensive voyage through a noisy and perplexing unknown. It sometimes takes days, even weeks, to become familiar with the campus, the rules you are expected to follow and where your place in all this bedlam happens to be. It can be a humbling, sometimes lonesome, experience. But if you can "imagine," at UBC first-year classes are cancelled and the day set aside to make first-year students feel at home, thanks to a campus-wide welcoming event.

Imagine UBC is UBC's innovative first-year orientation program—the largest of its kind in Canada. All first-year students participate in this official welcome, which offers help adjusting to university life, learning the layout of campus, learning about their faculties, where resources are located, who their fellow classmates are and what it means to be a UBC student.

New arrivals make new friends and meet with student leaders, professors and the Dean of their faculty. They learn about campus activities, clubs and opportunities available on campus. This is a program driven by students for students. Imagine UBC turns apprehension into fun, makes the Big seem Small, provides new students with a sense of direction and belonging, and teaches them that UBC is the best university in the country. It is perhaps not surprising that the student participation rate is well over 90 percent.

Imagine it was your first day of classes at UBC—and the classes were cancelled, for a day's fun, culminating in a rally in The War Memorial Gym.

Imagine UBC runs on the energy of MUGs ("My Undergraduate Group"), the term used to identify student leader volunteers (sophomores and beyond) and faculty-member volunteers who gather their first-year assignees in soon-to-be-familiar groups. On average, more than 800 UBC students volunteer for 500 MUG leader positions, a 12-month commitment that includes filling roughly 4,000 frosh kits with campus information and support material and steering the new students through workshops, familiarization sessions, pep rallies and even parties.

When the Imagine UBC day ends, the volunteer leaders keep first-year students up to date on what is happening at UBC on a regular basis. MUG leaders continue to check-in on their group members, answering questions and providing support when the need is there. In addition to making new students feel welcome at UBC, it is said the experience increases an already proud sense of volunteerism on campus, provides valuable leadership training and, in the long run, produces alumni with a greater fondness for their alma mater. In that sense, it is also said that at UBC, where enthusiasm and friendships easily thrive, "the first day lasts all year ... and beyond that, sometimes a lifetime."

On Day-One, help for first-year students can appear in the strangest manifestations.

Learning in paradise (above): first-year students head for the beach and settle in to their studies the day after Imagine UBC.

Classes get under way (left) in UBC's Science One mode. Interdisciplinary study has seldom been so casual, or so effective.

THE INTERNATIONAL STUDENT

FOR UBC STUDENTS, FACULTY AND STAFF to make significant contributions to the global society, they must have the chance to travel, study and work overseas. UBC's international exchange programs provide these opportunities. UBC is also strengthening its efforts to enrol more students from around the world and to provide increased support for eligible students facing financial barriers. UBC has 80 student-exchange programs with universities in 23 countries around the world. About one-half the students entering Arts speak a language other than English or French. UBC hosts a large number of students from Korea University. The opening of Korea University-UBC House in September 2002 signalled the beginning of a new initiative that will lead to the establishment of an International College at UBC. Tecnologico de Monterrey, the largest technical university in Mexico, and UBC are committed to the construction of Tec de Monterrey-UBC House, a residence to accommodate 175 students on campus scheduled to open in the 2003/04 academic year. A unique academic and cultural initiative with Ritsumeikan University in Kyoto, Japan, which began in 1991, already brings 100 Japanese students to UBC each year to live and study in an integrated academic and social environment. UBC students can gain international and intercultural experience while living at "Rits House" or by taking specially designed integrated courses. These initiatives are important steps toward fulfilling UBC's *Trek 2000* goal to strengthen the internationalization of the campus by increasing the number of students from around the world and by encouraging more Canadian students to enrol in study-abroad programs.

While most universities offer exchanges to students only in second or third year, students in the Faculty of Arts can spend their first year at the International Study Centre at Herstmonceaux Castle in England.

SUPER STUDENTS

Iulia Litman (below): "The best thing is the support I got from faculty and my colleagues at UBC ... They've been there step by step and that's why I'm here."

James Dai (opposite): "Technology should help people interact with each other, otherwise it's just bells and whistles."

UBC'S FIRST PRESIDENT, DR. FRANK WESBROOK, wrote enthusiastically at the end of the University's first academic year: "One cannot but be optimistic in Canada ... We have been so richly endowed in British Columbia that we owe it to ourselves and the rest of the world to properly conserve and intelligently develop and use our material resources, the chief of which are men and women, both those who are here now and those who are coming."

Each new UBC graduating class seems to justify Dr. Wesbrook's belief in the quality of student this University has attracted, and continues to attract to this day. Intelligent, poised, inquisitive, involved in their communities, resumés full with accomplishments and stories of personal and scholarly determination, they underscore Dr. Wesbrook's belief that we can only be optimistic about their future.

WHEN 10-YEAR-OLD JAMES DAI arrived in Vancouver from Qin Huang Dao, China, in 1990 he could not speak a word of English. Five years later he had completed elementary school, high school, enrolled at UBC and was studying Computer Science. In 2002, the B.Sc. graduate was on his way to MIT to learn how to better use computer technology to teach literacy to children. Driven by a deeply-felt passion for the theatre and the performing arts, Dai made his mark when he co-designed PrimeClimb, a computer game that bridges the gap between the power of the computer and human intelligence.

IN 1989, IULIA LITMAN longed to teach history, but the Communist regime in Romania at the time thought her family ties "too intellectual" to allow her to study history. Although disappointed, she opted to attend the Wood Industry Faculty at the University of Transylvania in Brasov. She completed three years of the demanding five-year program but left Romania for Canada in 1994 to follow her husband-to-be. It was a difficult move. She knew little English. She left family and friends behind. She worked at odd jobs to help support the family. Eventually she enrolled at UBC's Centre of Advanced Wood Processing. It took three more years to complete her Bachelor of Wood Science degree and graduate in 2002. The thought of teaching history is now a distant dream, but Iulia is without regrets. She now plans to pursue a Master's degree in Forestry.

YAA-HEMAA OBIRI-YEBOAH is British Columbia's 2003 Rhodes Scholar, an honour only available to students exhibiting a high level of literacy and scholastic achievement, proficiency in sports, strong leadership qualities and a record of public service. But the path to B.C. for the fourth-year English Honours major (with a minor in Political Science) was circuitous and not without its dangers. When Obiri Yeboah was six she and her family were forced to flee Ghana, after a coup d'état, and then Nigeria, before they arrived in Canada as refugees. Obiri-Yeboah quickly adapted to Canadian life. The now-21-year-old student achieved Grade 10 in piano, plays field hockey, has written articles for the *African News*, and worked as a peer counsellor and mentor. The 85-per-cent-average student was a member of the Golden Key Honours Society, the Black Cultural Association and a Bible studies social club. She was also involved in UBC student politics and writes and speaks on human rights and the plight of marginalized peoples. At Oxford University, B.C.'s Rhodes Scholar intended to pursue graduate studies in English, with a concentration on African studies. Other Rhodes Scholars include former Canadian Prime Minister (and UBC alumnus) John Turner and former U.S. President Bill Clinton.

TO A GREAT EXTENT, passion has dictated the direction Marnie Williston's academic career path has taken. Williston came to British Columbia in 1994 from England and worked in social services with the elderly, as well as with women and children in crisis. But she longed to study science—chemistry in particular—and worked hard to achieve a Bachelor of Applied Science degree in 2002, as well as a Wesbrook Scholar award. Still, the tug of social responsibility seems as strong as her love for chemistry. Williston has been president of the Chemical and Biological Engineering Student Club and acted as a speaker for Engineers Without Borders. She has worked to encourage other young people to explore careers in engineering and apply those skills to benefit people, particularly in developing countries. As a co-op student, she travelled to Japan and worked as a chemical engineer for a large cement company. On graduating she joined BP Canada Energy as a plant engineer.

Yaa-Hemaa Obiri-Yeboah: "I want to shatter stereotypes placed upon African peoples..I want to participate in this process of telling a new story about Africa and its people."

Marnie Williston: "I've had so many opportunities,
but the amazing thing is that I didn't have to look for them.
I just had to be aware and always willing to say 'yes'
at the right moment."

Green College (right), whose motto is "Ideas and Friendship," was founded in 1993 as a centre for advanced interdisciplinary scholarship. The College includes resident accommodation for 82 graduate students, 16 post-doctoral scholars and five short-term visitors, all chosen on the basis of excellence, interdisciplinary interests and a commitment to involve themselves in the life of the College in order to achieve a more diverse community.

St. John's College was established in 1997 as an international residential college for outstanding post-graduate students, post-doctoral fellows and visiting scholars. The College, built on an "internationalism" theme, is modelled on Shanghai's St. John's University, until 1952 an institute with a distinguished reputation for international study in business, medicine and architecture.

COLLEGES

UBC's FACULTY OF GRADUATE STUDIES has long been known for establishing and supporting programs that are imaginative in scope and vigorous in the application of academic standards. In these particular examples— Green College and St. John's College—the emphasis is on using the approaches and values of the past to lay stronger academic foundations for the future. In Green College, the goal is to build an intellectual community for the generation of new ideas best fostered by interdisciplinary activities. In St. John's, the intention is to build links between different parts of the world by sharing interests in advancing international research and global-change studies.

INTO THE COMMUNITY

IN 1922, UBC students, frustrated over the provincial government's refusal to restart construction at UBC's Point Grey site, marched in the "Great Trek" protest away from downtown Vancouver to the distant, unfinished barrens of Point Grey. Almost 80 years later, heeding a different public call—and accepting the mild irony that went with it—UBC turned back to the east and established a permanent downtown location at Robson Square to better serve the educational needs of the Greater Vancouver community.

Times change and today's mission calls for wider community involvement for UBC. The opening of "UBC at Robson Square" in November 2001 marked a significant initiative in the University's *Trek 2000* commitment to bring opportunities for lifelong learning, professional development and career advancement to the downtown core. It showed UBC's resolve to make higher education more accessible to a larger portion of the public by bringing new programs, knowledge and innovation right to their doorsteps.

The Learning Exchange is another innovative UBC community outreach program, this one located in the Downtown Eastside area of Vancouver. The role of the Learning Exchange is to foster connections between people at UBC and people in the Downtown Eastside. The Learning Exchange puts UBC at the forefront of Canadian university efforts to serve their communities by providing stimulating learning environments for a broader range of citizens.

The Downtown Eastside consists of a number of diverse neighbourhoods facing significant social, economic and health-related issues. The Learning Exchange provides educational and life-skill opportunities for people who live and work in the area, while at the same time providing opportunities for UBC students to develop—through hands-on, volunteer work—a part of their society they might not always be fully aware of, or properly understand.

The Trek volunteer program for the Learning Exchange involves more than 100 students participating in activities ranging from literacy tutoring and fine arts to hot lunch, recreation and hospice programs.

UBC at Robson Square contains 66,000 square feet of floor space on two levels. This downtown campus contains classrooms, computer labs, board and seminar rooms, and space for theatrical performances, offices and meetings.

FROM CLAY TABLETS TO BROADBAND

UBC's MAIN LIBRARY functions as the heart of a massive vascular system that coordinates and pumps information back and forth across the campus, into the community and around the globe. UBC's library—the second-largest research library in Canada—includes 21 branch libraries on campus, four off-campus libraries (three at teaching hospitals and one at the Robson Square downtown campus), houses more than four million books and journals and more than six million microforms, maps, videos and other multimedia materials. Two important initiatives will propel UBC's library system into the electronic future, significantly changing the concept of "the library."

The first was the introduction of the Chapman Learning Commons in the winter of 2002, a time-shift experience that changed the Main Library's concourse from a hall of catalogue cases and card files into a dynamic, high-technology learning space. The second initiative was scheduled to arrive in 2005 with the Irving K. Barber Learning Centre's introduction of Canada's first robotic book storage and retrieval system, as well as providing electronic access for users, equipping smart classrooms with the latest technology and introducing an expanded role as a research centre for the community, along with the UBC campus.

Libraries are the heart of great universities. They are where the knowledge chain begins, mysterious pockets of learning that blossom on discovery into information, then erudition and, finally, scholarship. They are where great ideas are born. A library can also be a place of quiet contemplation, a station of emotional escape and reflection that often helps clear personal paths, as Shakespeare put it, "to the dauntless spirit of resolution."

At UBC's inception, the concept of a stand-alone library was given short shrift. In 1912, when the provincial government deliberated over what kind of university to build, it began by blithely ignoring the need for a library, choosing instead buildings for Arts, Sciences, Agriculture, dormitories and a powerhouse. When Frank Wesbrook became UBC's first President the next year, one of his first actions was to ensure that a library was included in the initial group of buildings to be erected at Point Grey. The Library was one of only three permanent buildings constructed on the site. The Library consisted of only the central portion of the present Main Library building, but it came with 55,000 books, shelving for 135,000 volumes and study space for 350 students.

The Main Library carries a cute stonemason's hint at what year construction was completed. Two small carvings adorn the granite entrance. One resembles a Prohibitionist cartoon figure representing a Fundamentalist, labelled FUNDA. Another depicts an ape and is labelled EVOL. The year of final construction? Why, 1925, of course; the year of the famous Scopes, or "Monkey," trial. John Scopes was a Dayton, Tennessee, teacher arrested for teaching Darwin's theory of evolution.

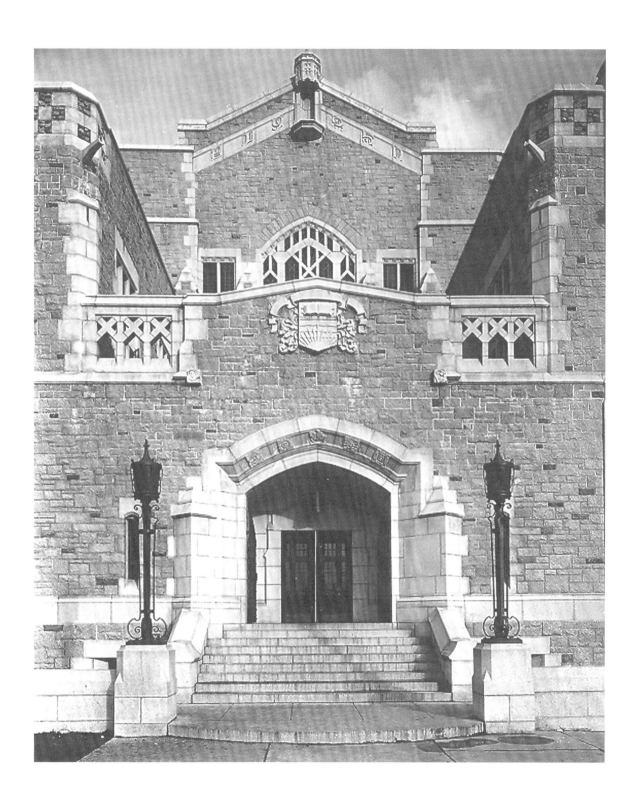

Sanders Phillips and Co., Ltd, THE BAYNARD PRESS, Chryssell Road, S.W.9

The UBC Library has, through the years, benefited significantly from the exceptional generosity of alumni and donors.

Two important collections received during the Library's formative years were the 1966 donation of The Norman Colbeck Collection—a unique gathering of 19th-century belles-lettres, monographs and English and Anglo-Irish poetry—and the 1965 donation of $3 million for library acquistions by long-time benefactor H.R. MacMillan. The MacMillan contribution transformed the Library and moved it into the ranks of the top research libraries in North America. Two more recent examples of this continuing generosity are The Wallace B. Chung and Madeline H. Chung Collection of Western Canadian memorabilia and The H. Colin Slim Stravinsky Collection (opposite).

UNIQUE AND INVALUABLE COLLECTIONS

THE CHUNG COLLECTION is a priceless research collection of more than 25,000 items and memorabilia about the exploration and settlement of the Pacific Northwest, the Chinese experience in North America and the story of the Canadian Pacific Railway Company in British Columbia. The collection is a donation of Dr. Wallace B. Chung, the retired Head of the Department of Surgery at the UBC Hospital, and his wife, Dr. Madeline H. Chung. The collection, given to the University in 1999, has been called "a national treasure" and "one of the most exceptional and extensive collections of its kind in North America."

ALTHOUGH HE DIED IN 1971, the legacy of Russian-born composer Igor Stravinsky lives on in the UBC Library's Special Collections section, thanks to a generous gift from alumnus H. Colin Slim, a prominent North American musicologist. The H. Colin Slim Stravinsky Collection contains more than 130 items that once belonged to the eminent composer. Dr. Slim's fascination with Stravinsky began as a UBC music student. "I gave the Collection to UBC because I feel much gratitude for the opportunities afforded me as an undergraduate," Dr. Slim said at the Collection's initial display in 2002.

ALINE FRUHAUF

THE KOERNER LIBRARY, described by architect Arthur Erickson as the "green jewel" of the University of British Columbia campus, was an instant landmark when it opened in March 1997. Situated with a central entry on axis with the historic Main Library building, the Koerner—with wired study spaces, on-line catalogues and a student computer lab—is an integral part of long-term redevelopment of the UBC library system. When renovation of the original building is complete in 2005, Main will become the Irving K. Barber Learning Centre, incorporating the latest in information technology and boasting an automated book retrieval system. UBC's library holdings range in format from Babylonian clay tablets to medieval manuscripts, oriental scrolls, CD-ROMs and an expanding collection of on-line resources.

THE KOERNER LIBRARY

Mr. Koerner, who passed away in July 1995, was born in 1898 in northern Moravia, now part of the Czech Republic. In 1938 he emigrated to Canada where he continued the family's centuries-old tradition of working in the forest industry. Mr. Koerner's association with UBC began in 1955 with a gift supporting the University's Slavonic Studies library collection. A year later he helped found the Friends of the University Library and in 1958 made a gift that enabled the Main Library to undertake a much-needed expansion. He initiated the UBC Health Sciences Centre project, the core pavilion of which is named after him, and chaired the Centre from 1971 to 1980. For his wide-ranging support and service to UBC, Mr. Koerner, a former Chairman of the Board of Governors, was recognized with an honorary degree in 1973. In 1994, the University announced that its new humanities and social science research library would be named after him.

Walter C. Koerner was a generous British Columbian who left a significant mark on education, health care and culture in his province. He was instrumental in the creation of UBC's Health Sciences Centre, the Museum of Anthropology, the Graduate Student Centre and the Library—including the establishment of several of its major collections. To honour his contribution to both the university and the community, UBC established Walter C. Koerner Graduate Fellowships.

FOOD FOR MIND AND BODY

ONE OF THE MOST IMPRESSIVE GOALS set by UBC's vision document for the 21st century, *Trek 2000*, is to enhance the University's performance and be recognized as the leading research university in Canada—as well as one of the leading research universities in the world. Support for that ambitious quest came in the form of a financial gift from Vancouver businessman Peter Wall. The Peter Wall Institute for Advanced Studies, located on the top floor of the University Centre at the north end of campus, was established in 1996 to support interdisciplinary research and creative activities expected to result in significant advances in knowledge. The first recipient of the Peter Wall Distinguished Professorship was the UBC Nobel Laureate, Dr. Michael Smith.

THE UBC BOOKSTORE, University-owned and -operated, is the largest academic bookstore in Western Canada. Proceeds from its operations support student services, facilities, programming and research. In addition to textbooks, bestsellers, new releases and magazines, the Bookstore offers a Discount Book Club, a Computer Shop, Alumni items, stationery supplies and crested sportswear—from sweaters to ball caps, from running shorts to "Bum Pants."

Located beneath the offices of the Networks of Centres of Excellence, and centrally located at East Mall and University Boulevard, the UBC Bookstore (above) acts, almost magnetically, as a point of convergence for students, faculty, staff and visitors.

The Sage Bistro (right) occupies the main floor of the former Faculty Club, now the University Centre, adjacent to the cultural heart of the campus. The Sage, open to the public as well as all members of the campus community, serves all meals complete with a view of Howe Sound, the North Shore mountains and Burrard Inlet.

MIND. BODY. SPIRIT

"Success in athletics works hand-in-hand with academic success to develop strong and well-rounded students and future community leaders."
—UBC PRESIDENT MARTHA PIPER

UBC'S FIRST CLASSES were barely under way in 1915 and women students were already organizing a field hockey team, while male students were rallying support for an ice hockey team, rugby competition and a swimming club. Interclass competition provided an important physical outlet for students, even though such games were often perceived, incorrectly, as diversions for idle and bored undergraduates. As competence grew out of competition, UBC teams began earning national and international reputations. In 1935/36, intramural competition was formally sanctioned in soccer, basketball and rugby, later to include touch football, lacrosse, curling, table tennis, bowling, golf, volleyball and ice hockey. Today, UBC's intramural sports and recreation program is Canada's largest and most successful. Now known as The Legacy Games, they have for decades enriched university life for students and faculty members, creating fun and companionship, and complementing the educational process to the benefit of the entire university community.

Today, UBC is represented around the world in university- and elite-level competition by 28 varsity Thunderbird sports teams in 15 different sports. UBC has won 52 national championships in sports (second only to the University of Toronto) ranging from football to swimming, golf to basketball. And UBC athletes have consistently performed exceptional feats in winning Olympic, British Empire and Commonwealth Games medals for Canada, beginning with Ned Pratt's Olympic bronze in double sculls in 1932.

In 1946, the UBC Thunderbirds rattled North American basketball circles when they upset the famed Harlem Globetrotters 42-38 in an exhibition match.

UBC pitcher Jeff Francis (right) made Canadian baseball history in 2001 when he was chosen as the Colorado Rockies' first-round draft choice. The physics major-cum-millionaire from North Delta, B.C., chose UBC baseball over U.S. colleges because of its emphasis on academics.

STUDENT RECREATION CENTRE

THE STUDENT RECREATION CENTRE—opened in 1995—contains the largest intramural sports and recreation program in Canada. The Centre houses an 8,000-square-foot fitness room and three large gymnasiums for a wide range of sports. The SRC can accommodate more than 1,500 students per day during peak periods. Over all, it is estimated that each year close to 50,000 students, faculty and community members take part in fitness and recreation activities at UBC.

THE UBC TEAM NAME, "THUNDERBIRDS," rings with all the symbolic power and fighting spirit of that famed west-coast mystery bird. According to UBC Athletics Historian Fred Hume, native mythology has it that Thunderbirds were creatures able to grant supernatural blessings or engage in warfare with the earth's most fierce beasts. With lightning for eyes, thundering wings and talons strong enough to lift a whale from the ocean, Thunderbirds were perfect visions of strength and fearlessness for competitive sports teams. But until the early 1930s UBC teams used a number of names—Varsity or the Blue and Gold were the most popular.

The SRC fitness facility (above)—known as "The Bird Coop"—offers fitness classes, personal training and fitness assessments, stress-management courses, martial arts—even ballroom dancing.

TEAMWORK

In late 1933, the *Ubyssey* held a contest to let students choose a permanent name. The students passed on Thunderbirds. They even passed on Golden Eagles. Oddly enough, they settled on Seagulls. Refusing to accept such a wimpy name for their sports teams, the *Ubyssey's* staff overruled the student body and arbitrarily chose Thunderbirds. At the 1948 Homecoming football game the Kwicksutaineuk people and Chief William Scow officially sanctioned use of the name of Thunderbird for campus teams. As part of the dedication ceremony, native carvers Ellen and Ted Neal presented to UBC a 22-foot totem pole which sanctified the occasion.

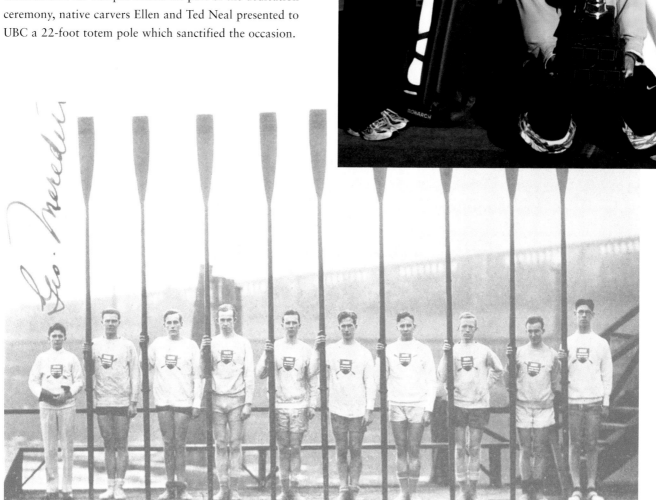

UBC's 2001 CIS National Champions
in Field Hockey (left).

Stalwart rowing crews, like this
one in 1929 (opposite) were the
foundation for UBC's emergence as
world champions in the 1950s.

An exhibition of UBC "teamwork"
on the Dance Club floor (right) .

Thunderbird Stadium (below) is the
campus venue for varsity football,
soccer, international rugby and the
occasional rock concert.

As IMPRESSIVE as the individual performances of UBC athletes have been at national and international levels, often the most thrilling achievements have come from UBC Thunderbird teams. In 1930 the Senior "A" Women's basketball won a World Championship at the Women's International Games. In 1954, UBC rowers triggered the University's "Golden Age of Rowing" when the men's eight-oared crew defeated heavily favoured England for the gold medal at the British Empire Games. In 1955, at the Henley Regatta, the UBC team upset the defending champions from the Soviet Union and followed that major success by winning an Olympic gold medal in fours, and a silver in the eights, at the 1956 Olympic Games in Melbourne. The 1966/67 men's volleyball team revolutionized the game in Canada when it became the first volleyball team to win the CIS National Championships. UBC's women's basketball team were Canadian champions in 1969/70, while the men's team won national championships in 1970 and 1972. And in 2002 both the Thunderbird women's and men's swim teams made Canadian athletic history, winning their fifth dual national championship in a row. It was the first time a university had won five consecutive Canadian Interuniversity Sport championships, by both women and men, in a single sport.

THE UBC HALL OF FAME acknowledges UBC's outstanding athletes and their accomplishments, builders of UBC sports activities, and some of the most successful Thunderbird teams. Located in the foyer of the War Memorial Gymnasium, the Hall of Fame serves to maintain student, faculty and alumni awareness of how much these individuals have contributed to the University's rich athletic history.

Bobby Gaul (1930s Rugby, Track): A superior athlete who best combined qualities of leadership and scholarship, and of whom it was once said: "He was one of those rare and lovely souls in whom one would wish to see no change."

Marilyn Peterson-Kinghorn (1950s/60s Basketball, Track): "An amazing all-around athlete" who led UBC teams to four Western Canadian titles (two in basketball, one in track and one in volleyball), exemplifying scholarship, leadership and service.

Gordon "Cokie" Shields (1920s Tennis, Track, Football, Rugby, Soccer and Badminton): "A star in the real sense," probably UBC's most multitalented athlete.

Reg Clarkson (1940s Basketball, Football): One of the province's most versatile athletes. Starred in basketball with the 1945/46 Hall of Fame team and went on to play professional baseball, football and basketball.

Tricia Smith (1980s Rowing): One of Canada's most internationally medalled athletes: seven world championships, Commonwealth gold medal, Olympic silver, only UBC athlete selected to represent Canada at four Olympic Games—1976, 1980, 1984, 1988.

Jeannie Cockcroft (1980s Track): Three-time CIAU national high jump champion and the most successful female high jumper in Canadian university history. Twice UBC's Female Athlete of the Year.

Frank Gnup (Builder): A coach, mentor, character builder and "Mr. Thunderbird" to everyone who knew him as coach of the UBC football team from 1955 to 1973. Gnup also coached baseball and golf, in addition to football, where his teams won three Hardy Cups.

The 1948/50 UBC Hockey Team: the first team to be inducted into the UBC Hall of Fame; defeated Western Canadian champions (University of Alberta) to win the inaugural Hamber Cup.

UBC athletes form the "Thunderbird"—with Hall of Famer George Puil on top (opposite).

UBC women's soccer team—the 2002 CIS National Championships (right).

Yesteryear's athletic stars attend the launch of the UBC Sports Hall of Fame and its website in 2002 (below, left to right): Mary Campbell, a member of UBC's world-champion 1930 basketball team; Bob Hindmarch, Director Emeritus of Athletics and Hall of Famer; Lois Fisher, another player on the 1930 team; and Chancellor Allan McEachern, who played football and rugby at the University.

The UBC women's basketball team of 1939-40 (bottom), including Hall of Famers Jean Bardsley (second from right) and Ruth Wilson (third from right).

BREAKFAST OF CHAMPIONS

THANKS TO THE EFFORTS AND CONTRIBUTIONS of Alumni and community supporters—and with matching funds from UBC—in only four years the Thunderbird Millennium Breakfast program has raised an endowment fund of roughly $2 million for student athlete scholarships. The program is aimed at attracting, and retaining, exceptional athletes to UBC. Each year more than 1,500 patrons gather for the annual breakfast. The Thunderbird Millennium Breakfast is the most successful community fundraising event staged by a university athletic program in Canada.

Both men's and women's basketball teams from UBC have won national championships over the years.

World-record-breaking UBC swimmer
and Arts student Brian Johns (above)
strokes his way to the Outstanding
Male Swimmer award for 2002—
the sixth male swimmer in UBC
history to take the national award.

A "training session" at the UBC
Aquatic Centre (right)—after the sun
comes out from behind the clouds.

Light upon light at midday

The Main Mall between classes

Housed in a richly symbolic building, with calm surroundings and enveloping concrete pools (above), the Asian Centre reflects the strong, growing spirit of cooperation and friendship between UBC and Asian educational institutions.

A world of its own: the Museum of Anthropology (opposite) anchors the vista of the University as seen from the Strait of Georgia.

THE SOPRON LEGACY

The most impressive feature of the inner atrium of the Forest Sciences Building (opposite) is its clustered Parallam beams reaching four storeys to the glass ceiling above. It is like walking into a mature forest. You expect to hear bird song and the sighing of breezes.

In 1957 students and faculty of Hungary's Sopron School of Forestry (below) resettled at UBC's Faculty of Forestry.

WHEN SOVIET TROOPS invaded Hungary in 1956, they sparked an academic emigration that helped transform UBC's Faculty of Forestry from a struggling, five-year-old facility into one of the foremost forestry schools in North America.

Many Hungarian students of the 200-year-old Sopron School of Forestry attempted resistance against the Soviet tanks, but their efforts proved futile and about 250 students, faculty and their families were forced to cross the border into Austria. When it became clear to them that a return to their homeland was impossible, letters were sent to a number of countries explaining their plight and the need to emigrate. Of a number of responses, the one from Canada—specifically the University of British Columbia—was the most attractive.

When UBC's Faculty of Forestry opened in 1951 there were only three similar schools in the country, and the industry faced a shortage of trained foresters. To make matters worse, management practices were outdated and the absence of proper environmental procedures was a major issue with industry critics. George Allen, UBC Dean of Forestry at the time, believed that universities needed to train a new generation of forester to ensure long-term growth and prosperity. Dean Allen was aware of the Sopron School's predicament and saw it as an opportunity to increase UBC's talent base while offering sanctuary for the men and women displaced by the Soviet invasion. With the backing of UBC's then-President, Norman MacKenzie, and with the help of the federal government, Dean Allen offered to accept 200 Sopron students and 14 faculty members for five years. It was an incredible coup for Dean Allen and his department. In one gesture, UBC had its "new generation," symbolized by this unorthodox infusion of talent and energy.

BUILDING SUSTAINABLE U

"SUSTAINABILITY" is defined on the UBC campus as the ability to achieve a balance between ecological, economic and societal goals. There is no doubt that UBC is the national role model for meeting university sustainability challenges. Canada's west coast has long been receptive to environmental protection. In 1970, when the Greenpeace movement was organized (originally named the Don't Make a Wave Committee) to stop U.S. underground nuclear testing at Amchitka, a tiny island off the west coast of Alaska, two of the five committee organizers were UBC students.

In 1998, UBC opened the first Campus Sustainability Office in Canada. The results have been impressive. Since the CSO's introduction, UBC has saved roughly $2 million by recycling paper, monitoring electricity utilization, controlling water use and implementing environmentally friendly design functions into all new construction on campus. Interestingly enough, even though UBC's population is increasing dramatically and building construction is moving at a furious pace, consumption of electricity on campus is decreasing. Since 1992, UBC has made green-building targets a part of all new building projects.

Ideally, UBC's sustainability initiatives should establish a strong role model for other educational institutions attempting to meet sustainable goals. UBC is working to incorporate sustainability into its teaching, research and operations down to grassroot levels. Students are encouraged to take Sustainability Pledges. The SEEDS program coordinates internships and applied research opportunities relating to sustainability. Sustainability Circles are organized semi-annually to enhance networking and communications.

Dr. John Robinson (left) of the Sustainable Development Research Institute established the Greening the Campus initiative in 1994 (now SEEDS: Social, Ecological, Economic Development Seeds). From 1994 to 1998, students researched and produced over 50 projects related to campus sustainability.

David Suzuki (above), retired UBC zoology professor and host of CBC Television's The Nature of Things, has been widely credited for having popularized science and sensitized Canadians to a broad range of important environmental issues.

UBC's Campus Sustainability Office's director, Freda Pagani (opposite), has been given the go-ahead for a $35-million ECOTrek to upgrade UBC buildings. The result could see CO_2 emissions reduced by 30,000 tons a year, water use by 30 percent and energy use by 45 percent.

RECOGNIZED by the American Institute of Architects as one of its Top Ten Earth Day 2000 Green Buildings, with its wave-like roof design and daringly innovative architecture—inside and out—UBC's C.K. Choi building has set an international benchmark in sustainable building design and construction. More than one-half of the building's construction material is recycled, including reused timber from the University's dismantled 70-year-old Armouries building. Inside, composting toilets eliminate the need for water for sewage treatment, and grey water is collected in the building and directed outside for the irrigating of adjacent gardens—saving over 1,500 gallons of potable water daily. Automatic controls dim lights if adequate daylight is available, or turn off lights if a room is vacant. Natural ventilation instead of a traditional ducted air system saves equivalent energy to that needed to power four Vancouver homes for a year.

The late Dr. C.K. Choi was a longtime friend and supporter of UBC.

A PLACE OF QUIET BEAUTY

THE CROWN PRINCE OF JAPAN, on a visit to UBC's renowned Nitobe Memorial Garden, reacted almost breathlessly when he first laid eyes on the Garden: "I am in Japan!" he exclaimed in wonderment. The Nitobe Garden, constructed in 1960 in honour of Dr. Inazo Nitobe, is a striking work of landscape art that almost defies time and space. Carved out of a tract of the lush conifer forest that surrounds the UBC campus, this hectare of sublime, transplanted culture pays homage to Dr. Nitobe, a Japanese scholar, international diplomat and friend of the University of British Columbia. Dr. Nitobe's life was a personal quest for peace and international cooperation in the early years of the 20th century. His goal was "to be the connecting bridge over the Pacific Ocean," between Japan and his North American friends and fellow educators.

The Nitobe Garden is a gentle symbol of UBC's enduring role as a leading academic window on Japan and other Asia Pacific countries. Asian students have long been welcomed at the University, signified these days by exciting student-exchange programs launched with Japan's Ritsumeikan University, Korea University and numerous other Pacific Rim universities. In fact, Dr. Nitobe's "connecting bridge" has turned out to be a vibrant, growing two-way structure. In the last five years of the 20th century, student enrolment in UBC's Japanese-language program tripled to more than 1,400 students. UBC now has the largest Japanese-language program in continental North America and the largest first-year classical-language course outside of Japan.

The Nitobe Memorial Garden is an authentic Shinto Stroll Garden, complete with ceremonial Tea House and inner Zen Garden. It is considered to be the best traditional example of the Shinto Garden in North America.

UBC's Botanical Garden, 28 hectares of magnificent gardens and plants situated at the extreme southwest section of the campus, harbours the finest rhododendron and Asian plant collections in North America.

DATING BACK TO 1916, the Botanical Garden is both the oldest department on campus and the first university botanical garden in Canada. The Botanical Garden consists of three main sites: the main Garden; the Botanical Garden Nursery; and the Nitobe Memorial Garden. Among the foremost attractions are the 15-hectare David C. Lam Asian Garden and the E.H. Lohbrunner Alpine Garden. The Alpine Garden displays small and unusual plants in a stunning one-hectare mountainside setting. The Asian Garden—named for the Honourable David C. Lam, B.C.'s first Chinese-Canadian Lieutenant Governor—includes more than 500 species, subspecies, varieties and forms of rhododendrons alone.

ACROSS THE BUSY UBC CAMPUS it can sometimes seem difficult to find a quiet place to pause and reflect, or just escape long enough to read a page or two of a good book. There are such serene places on campus, many of them squirreled away so well they can hardly be discovered. Not many can be found amid wide-open spaces.

But UBC's Rose Garden, situated at the northwest extreme
of the Main Mall, between the University Centre and the
Chan Centre for the Performing Arts, is just such a place.

Bathed in sunlight or tempered with cloud, the Rose
Garden offers students, faculty and visitors alike an
opportunity to capture moments of contemplative pleasure
and, at the same time, savour one of nature's finest vistas—
the view that overlooks the magnificent Strait of Georgia
and takes in the towering backdrop of the North Shore
mountains. From the Rose Garden, one quickly is immersed
in the most spectacular outdoor view on campus.

"YOU AND I"

TENTH ANNUAL PERFORMANCE OF THE UNIVERSITY

PLAYERS CLUB

MISS OENONE BAILLIE — BETTY

MISS BICE CLEGG — NANCY

MR. PETER PRICE — MAITEY

MISS BAILLIE & MR. KENNETH CAPLE

MISS B. CLEGG & MR. P. PRICE

MR. HARRY WARREN — G.T. WARREN

ORPHEUM THEATRE
MARCH 16TH 17TH & 18TH
MON TUES WED

PHOTOGRAPHS

CHARLES WEST

GREASEPAINT AND DEGREES

"To the people we met here, theatre really mattered. It made us feel that it was the best, the bravest, the finest thing you could do with your life..."
— Actress Nicola Cavendish,
  UBC Alumna

THE FREDERIC WOOD THEATRE stands as a tribute to the man whose name is synonymous with the development of theatre in British Columbia. Born in Victoria in 1887, "Freddy" Wood earned an M.A. from Harvard University and, in 1915, became the first B.C. male appointed to the faculty of the University of British Columbia. That same year he and 40 students formed the Players' Club—the first, and longest-running, all-student drama society in Canada and one that quickly became the social and intellectual heart of the campus. It laid the foundation for the present UBC Theatre Department. Over the years, Freddy Wood also directed more than 30 theatrical productions across the province. He retired from UBC in

1950 as the longest-serving original staff member, although even after his retirement he continued to assume an active interest in the theatre until his death in 1976. A first Frederic Wood Theatre was constructed in 1952, and in September 1963, the current 410-seat theatre was opened to much praise for its excellent acoustics and proscenium design.

In late 2002, a gala reunion was held at UBC to mark the 50th year since the construction of the first Freddy Wood Theatre. Notable alumni in attendance included Brent Carver, Nicola Cavendish, Eric Peterson and John MacLachlan Gray. Lysistrata (right), 2001/02, with Jessica Clements.

THE MORRIS AND HELEN BELKIN GALLERY

UBC's FINE ARTS GALLERY was founded in 1948 and located in the basement of the Main Library. Its first director, B.C. Binning, was also the first head of UBC's Fine Arts Department. Binning put in place an innovative, contemporary art program that was unmatched by any Canadian university. For much of the 1960s and 1970s UBC achieved a national profile with venturesome exhibitions of contemporary art. These "avant garde narratives," as they are referred to, included the work of Peter Day, Michael Morris and Vincent Trasov. In 1995, the gallery opened new premises on Main Mall, rededicated as the Morris and Helen Belkin Art Gallery. The Gallery's collection now contains more than 2,000 artworks, making it the third-largest public collection in the province. It includes works by Emily Carr, Jock Macdonald, the Group of Seven's Fred Varley, as well as pieces by Attila Lukacs, Roy Arden, Jeff Wall and American artist, Jess. The Gallery also holds more than 20,000 archival items relating to the post-war history of art in Vancouver.

What's it all about...? The purpose of the Belkin Gallery is not only to exhibit and collect art. The Gallery's programs emphasize research, teaching and scholarship in areas ranging from B.C. art history to international perspectives in the arts.

THE CHAN CENTRE

FOR THE

PERFORMING ARTS

SINCE ITS OPENING in spring 1997, the Chan Centre for the Performing Arts has earned accolades for its striking design and exceptional acoustics. Designed by prominent Vancouver architect Bing Thom, it has been called "one of the world's greatest concert halls." Amid the lush landscape adjacent to the Rose Garden, the Chan's distinctive cylindrical shape has become a noted landmark. Inside, the Chan offers three unique venues: the 1,200-seat Chan Shun Concert Hall (named after the patriarch of the Chan family who helped fund the project); the Telus Studio Theatre; and the Royal Bank Cinema. All three share an elegant glass lobby that captures the tranquility of the surrounding evergreens and provides a stimulating and inviting entry to performances within. Canada's Governor-General, Adrienne Clarkson, was so impressed with the Chan Centre that she chose it as the locale for the first Order of Canada investiture to be held outside the National Capital. The Chan's mandate is to meet the artistic and performance needs of the UBC community and to provide for local and visiting arts enthusiasts an acoustically superior concert hall. Among the world-famous artists who have performed at the Chan are American soprano Renée Fleming, the Kronos Quartet and the legendary violin virtuoso Isaac Stern.

MUSIC: THE FOOD OF LOVE

THE SCHOOL OF MUSIC at the University of British Columbia is the largest of its kind in Western Canada and one of the biggest in Canada. It has, from its beginning, been home to the performance of music as well as the study of music. The program is based on the belief that it is not enough for violinists, pianists and singers to learn to perform well. They must be broadly educated, with a thorough foundation in the study of music and with a knowledge of, and appreciation for, the liberal arts.

Classical musicians rehearse at the Chan Centre (above); the UBC Opera Ensemble performs Mozart's Die Gärtneren aus Liebe *(right).*

The Borealis String Quartet (right) is four young, gifted musicians—violinists Patricia Shih and Yuel Yawney, violist Nikita Pogrebnoy and cellist Joel Stobbe— who are the first participants in a professional quartet-in-residence program offered at a Canadian university.

THE STUDY OF MUSIC was introduced at UBC as early as 1935 with noon-hour lectures and recitals. The faculty committee that met in 1946 to discuss the establishment of a Chair of Music agreed that the University needed a wide variety of music and musicology: popular, non-credit lectures; authoritative lectures on the history and theory of music for credit; and public performances of music that would benefit the University and the community at large. Noted Canadian violinist Harry Adaskin was chosen as the Head of the new Department of Music.

The result has been a wealth of student development and artistic performance. Today, the School of Music is recognized as the artistic cradle for such notable international opera stars as Ben Heppner and Judith Forst, and the home of such celebrated faculty performers as pianists Jane Coop and Robert Silverman and violinist Andrew Dawes. The School sponsors, on average, more than 100 ensemble, orchestral and operatic performances each year: from free noon-hour student recitals to evening performances in the Chan Centre for the Performing Arts; from free jazz to Pacific Spirit Concerts; from Bramwell Tovey conducting the Vancouver Symphony Orchestra to return performance visits by alumnus performer Jon Kimura Parker.

Nancy Hermiston is Head of the Voice and Opera Division at the UBC's School of Music: "Music is a particular way of communicating, of thinking, an art that transcends language differences and perceptions."

Back to the Future: UBC Music in the 1950s (above).

Robert Silverman (left) has been a faculty member since 1973 and served as the Director of the School of Music from 1991 to 1995. He is a renowned pianist who reached the peak of classical music in performing live and recording Beethoven's thirty-two piano Sonatas.

Tenor Ben Heppner (opposite) began his musical studies at UBC and went on to star on the worldwide opera scene with leading roles at La Scala, The Royal Opera Covent Garden and the Metropolitan Opera.

Jane Coop (right) is one of Canada's most celebrated pianists, an artist who has toured extensively around the globe and of whom it was written: "Coop has that extra something that lets a pianist become a poet."

Judith Forst (left), a UBC student in the early 1960s, has been called by The New York Times "one of the few truly world-class coloratura mezzos on the operatic stage."

Vancouver-born Arthur Erickson is recognized around the globe for his architectural accomplishments. In addition to UBC's brilliant Museum of Anthropology, Erickson has designed Simon Fraser University, the Canadian Pavilion at Osaka, Vancouver's Robson Square and Law Courts, the Roy Thompson Concert Hall in Toronto and the Canadian Embassy in Washington.

THE MUSEUM OF ANTHROPOLOGY

THE MUSEUM OF ANTHROPOLOGY is, in the world of exhibits, antiquities and anthropology, the University of British Columbia's jewel in the crown. Considered by many to be an architectural masterpiece, the spectacular Museum, designed by acclaimed Canadian architect Arthur Erickson, is, from the outside, a series of massive concrete posts and beams connected by glass, its form inspired by Northwest Coast Native construction. Inside, visitors are greeted by a stunning display of one of the world's outstanding collections of Northwest Coast First Nations art and artifacts, used for teaching and research as well as display purposes. The Museum sits majestically on the Point Grey promontory, surveying all that makes British Columbia so unique in setting and natural beauty: limitless vistas of mountains, sea, forests and protean skies.

The Museum's mission is to investigate, preserve and present objects and expressions of human creativity in order to promote understanding of, and respect for, world cultures. The MOA's Great Hall features a wide array of works by First Nations artists. Of special note, the MOA houses the world's largest collection of Bill Reid art and is the public institution most closely associated with him. Where Arthur Erickson serves as a world-renowned master of architectural expression, Reid is considered Canada's greatest native artist.

Sculptor Bill Reid carved his famous Haida Bear out of a single giant block of red cedar.

The Talking Stick (opposite) was used in native cultures when important issues needed to be discussed. Each individual who had something to contribute waited his or her turn to take possession of the Talking Stick and speak without interruption.

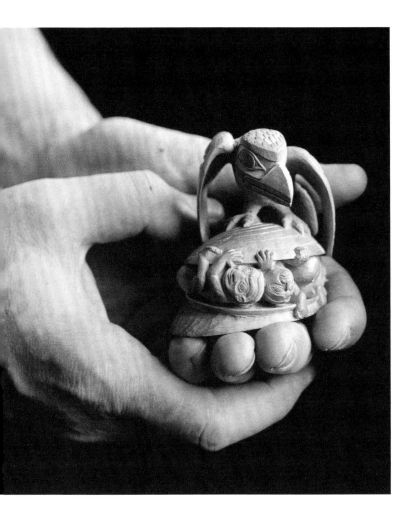

BILL REID was a world-celebrated Canadian sculptor, artist and craftsman. He was born in Victoria, B.C. in 1920 of a father of Scottish and German origin and a mother who was native-born Haida from the Queen Charlotte Islands. He was living in Toronto when he began to explore his Haida cultural heritage and the art of his people. When Reid returned from Eastern Canada, he began an association with UBC that spanned 40 years. In 1958, he was commissioned to create part of an authentic Haida village for the University. It was a turning point in his artistic career. The Haida village, which consisted of two houses, mortuary poles and totems, gave UBC's "Totem Park" its name; these objects now stand outside the MOA. The Haida village was first in a series of large-scale works for which Reid is best known. He constructed many masterpieces, including The Skidegate Pole in 1978, the First Men yellow cedar sculpture for the MOA in 1980, the Lord of the Under Sea bronze sculpture for the Vancouver Aquarium in 1984, the Lootas cedar canoe for Expo 86 and, most recently, two Spirit of Haida G'waii bronze, 19-foot sculptures. One is located at the Canadian Embassy in Washington, D.C., the other at the Vancouver International Airport. Before he died in 1998, Bill Reid was awarded eight honorary doctoral degrees, including one from UBC.

Two examples of Bill Reid art: his astonishing depiction of The Birth of Mankind (as a model, above left, and a full-sized sculpture, opposite), and an exquisite golden box.

The Museum of Anthropology is now home to a world-class collection of Chinese antiquities thanks to the generous donation of prominent collector Victor Shaw.

As the largest teaching museum in Canada, the MOA serves an important educational function—in museum studies, anthropology, archaeology, fine arts and conservation. As an interdisciplinary research installation, it links scholars, First Nations communities and research museums. The MOA has enormous public drawing power. Each year it is visited by more than 170,000 students, researchers, school children and tourists. It offers over 100 public programs annually, including tours, school programs, theatrical and musical performances, lectures and workshops.

Totem poles are among the most popular items at the MOA. They have been carved and raised for a variety of reasons, but usually to symbolize honour and prestige of family members. Some poles display myths and ancient story-telling. Cedar dugout canoes, with their distinctive, high-projecting bows and sterns, were once used for travel, fishing and whaling along the rugged Pacific coast. Traditional bentwood boxes, used for storage, ceremonies, cradles, even coffins, are displayed for their unique artistry.

UBC has collected ethnographic materials since 1927. Approximately 30,000 ethnographic objects and 200,000 archaeological objects are now housed within the Museum. In 1947, this material was brought together to form the founding collections of the MOA, then situated in the Main Library. The materials were moved to the current MOA in 1976. The construction of the new museum was made possible by a grant from the Government of Canada and UBC, and by Walter and Marianne Koerner's gift of their extensive Northwest Coast First Nations art collection.

A HOME AWAY FROM HOME

The magnificent First Nations Longhouse, built in 1993, is the home of the First Nations House of Learning. Built of western red cedar, with a copper-clad roof, it was based on traditional Coast Salish design. The mandate of the First Nations House of Learning is to make the University's resources more accessible to First People and to improve UBC's ability to meet the needs of First Nations—a term meant to refer to all people of aboriginal ancestry. The Longhouse is considered "a home away from home"—a structure within which First Nations students can study and learn in surroundings which reflect their traditions and cultures.

Funded by UBC's World of Opportunity Campaign and the Province of British Columbia, the Longhouse reflects the high priority that UBC places on the successes and achievements of First Nations students. Within the Longhouse, students have access to a library, lounge and computer laboratory, and they receive assistance on admission and counselling. They can take advantage of child-care facilities or join in academic or social functions held in the majestic Great Hall, or Sty-Wet-Tan.

Students in the First Nations House of Learning (above) can share their knowledge and culture with one another and the wider community.

The logo of the First Nations House of Learning (opposite), created by Tsimshian artist Glen Wood, is the split Raven, shaped as a house, and symbolic of the Raven transforming the University to reflect First Nations cultures and philosophies.

CECIL GREEN PARK HOUSE

CECIL GREEN PARK HOUSE was one of the first
fashionable homes in Vancouver's prestigious Point Grey
neighbourhood. Built in 1912 by architect Samuel
Maclure for Edward Davis, a prominent Canadian Pacific
Railway lawyer, Cecil Green Park House was originally
named "Kanakla," a West Coast native word meaning
"house on the cliff." Later owners named the majestic
Tudor mansion "Langara" and "Yorkeen." In 1966,
when Dr. Cecil H. Green and his wife, Ida—both major
benefactors to the University of British Columbia—made
the acquisition possible for UBC, the building was
renamed Cecil Green Park House.

A UBC alumnus who studied liberal arts and applied
science from 1918 to 1921, and then attended the
Massachusetts Institute of Technology to complete
bachelor's and master's degrees, Dr. Green was co-
founder of Geophysical Services Ltd., the company that
gave rise to Texas Instruments.

Cecil Green Park House now contains the University
of British Columbia's Public Affairs Office and Alumni
Association Office. It was Dr. Green's wish that the home
be used to foster closer "town-and-gown" relationships
between the university and the citizens it serves.

Cecil Green supported post-secondary education across
Canada, the United States and the United Kingdom.
He received honorary degrees from more than a dozen
universities, including UBC and Oxford. He was knighted
by Queen Elizabeth in 1991.

The elegant mansion, with its splendid view of the Strait of Georgia and the North Shore mountains, has become a popular venue for public receptions, weddings, banquets, meetings and other social events—including Mother's Day Tea. In 1989, the house and grounds were used in the Hollywood film Cousins, *starring Ted Danson and Isabella Rossellini.*

The Commodore Ballroom was the site of the 1933
Xmas eve Alumni dinner. UBC Alumni held annual
dinner dances throughout the 1920s and 1930s.

OUTSTANDING ALUMNI

UBC GRADUATES have gone on to become respected and influential members of their communities. They have established themselves professionally and built national and international reputations in fields as varied as the sciences, athletics, business, medicine, the performing arts, law, politics and government. The imposing list includes two Prime Ministers of Canada, a number of British Columbia premiers, two Nobel Laureates and a Chief Justice of the Supreme Court of Canada.

An important moment of educational transition takes place when a graduate walks across the stage during the convocation ceremony and pauses before the Chancellor, who taps the graduate on the head and says: "I admit you." The graduate then continues on across the stage, no longer a student, now a proud alumna or alumnus.

In 2002, more than 8,000 students made the transition from undergraduate to graduate, from postgraduate to the world of work. Since the Alumni Association was formed in 1915, more than 208,000 students have graduated from UBC. More than 152,000 graduates, living in 120 countries, remain in touch with their alma mater.

Author Pierre Berton (top) and former
Prime Ministers John Turner and Kim Campbell.

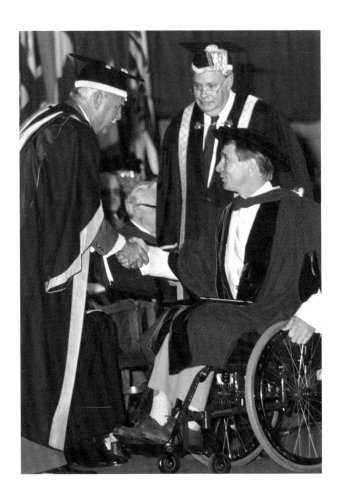

RICK HANSEN is a distinguished UBC alumnus, Honorary Degree holder and legendary Canadian who makes a habit of overcoming barriers others deem insuperable. At the age of 15 he was declared to be a paraplegic who would never walk again after a severe auto accident. By his early 20s he was an elite athlete, had graduated from UBC in Physical Education and had trekked 40,000 kilometres around the world in his wheelchair in a "Man-in-Motion" tour that raised $24 million for spinal cord injury research. By 2003, Hansen's efforts resulted in the establishment of the International Collaboration on Repair Discovery (ICORD), a multi-million-dollar spinal research facility—a partnership between UBC, the Vancouver General Hospital and the Province—giving new hope for those living with paralysis.

In their youth: federal cabinet minister David Anderson, mezzo-soprano Judith Forst, British Columbia Premier Mike Harcourt and Arts Club Theatre director Bill Millerd.

Pierre Berton: author, historian, broadcaster (B.A.41, D.LITT.85)

Rt. Hon. Kim Campbell: Prime Minister (B.A.69, LL.B.83, LL.D.00)

Kathleen Heddle: Olympic rower/gold medalist '92 and '96 (B.A.90)

Mike Harcourt: B.C. Premier (B.A.65, LL.B.68)

Robert Mundell: economist, awarded 1999 Bank of Sweden Prize in Economic Sciences in honour of Alfred Nobel (B.A.53, D.LITT.00)

Rt. Hon. John Turner: Prime Minister (B.A.49, LL.D.94)

Rosemary Brown: first black woman elected to a provincial legislature (M.S.W.67)

Ujjal Dosanjh: B.C. Premier (LL.B.76)

Madeleine Thien: writer, author (B.A.01)

Allan Fotheringham: journalist, author (B.A.54)

George Bowering: author, writer, poet and first national poet laureate (B.A.60, M.A.63)

Bill Millerd: playwright, theatre director (B.A.65)

Milton Wong: Chancellor, Simon Fraser University (B.A.63)

Bjarni Tryggvason: Canadian astronaut, first Icelander in space (B.A.Sc.72, D.LITT.00)

Allan Fotheringham (above right) working at the Ubyssey; *Novelist Madeleine Thien (right).*

THE TONE OF DYLAN THOMAS'S VISIT to UBC in April 1950 was captured in a letter to his wife, Caitlin Thomas: "Today is Good Friday, I am writing this in a hotel bedroom in Vancouver, British Columbia, Canada, where yesterday I gave two readings, one in the university, and one in the ballroom of the Vancouver Hotel, and made one broadcast. Vancouver is on the sea, and gigantic mountains doom above it ... Everyone is pious and patriotic, apart from a few people in the university ... "

CELEBRATED VISITORS

IN OCTOBER 1968, American Yippie leader Jerry Rubin visited the UBC campus and instigated both a pig-for-president candidacy and a 24-hour sit-in at the Faculty Club. Rubin suggested UBC students should adopt the American radical's slogan: "I say do this, do that. Whenever you see a rule, break it." The students spent their 24 hours drinking faculty liquor, smoking their cigarettes, doing dope, burning an American flag and swimming nude in the patio pool—"basically enjoying themselves" as the *Ubyssey* reported.

UNITED STATES PRESIDENT BILL CLINTON visited UBC twice, in 1993 for a geopolitical Summit Meeting with Russian President Boris Yeltsin, and in 1997 to attend the Asia-Pacific Economic Cooperation summit. President Clinton declared himself "enchanted" by UBC's Museum of Anthropology, in particular the sculpture of Bill Reid.

Among many guests who have visited the University over the years were Eleanor Roosevelt (to open International House in 1959), Beat poet Allen Ginsberg, His Royal Highness, the Prince of the Netherlands, poet W.H. Auden, free spirit Jerry Rubin (left), composer Aaron Copland, architect Eero Saarinen and anthropologist Margaret Mead.

Her Majesty in conversation with UBC President Martha Piper during Queen Elizabeth's and the Duke of Edinburgh's Royal Visit to British Columbia in October 2002. Over the past 50 years, the Royal Couple has made four visits to UBC's campus: in October 1951 for Homecoming; in July 1959 to open the new Faculty Club; in 1983 to visit the Museum of Anthropology, the Asian Centre and the Health Sciences Centre Hospital; and in 2002 as part of their Golden Jubilee Tour.

CONGREGATION

UBC's first Convocation ceremony took place on May 4, 1916, in the Hotel Vancouver ballroom. There were 41 graduates. UBC's first graduate degrees were conferred in 1919. UBC students now graduate from 12 faculties: Agricultural Sciences, Applied Science, Arts, Commerce and Business Administration, Dentistry, Education, Forestry, Graduate Studies, Law, Medicine, Pharmaceutical Sciences and Science.

More than 5,000 gowns and mortar boards are used for UBC's Convocation. Evolved from clothing worn by European scholars in the Middle Ages, the hoods and gowns are lined with colours that indicate the degree to be conferred. Members of the Convocation processions also wear colourful academic regalia from around the world, signifying their university of graduation and highest degree awarded.

Each year since 1919, UBC's graduating class has planted a tree to mark the occasion. The class of 2002 planted a zelcova tree near the Chan Centre of the Performing Arts, where the University of British Columbia's convocation now takes place.

The cameras come out to record one of the most important moments in a student's lifetime. The memories of years of study, toil and—occasionally—anguish quickly fade, replaced with a sense of triumph, the zip-click of a camera shutter and a nervous walk across the stage.

*"I knew a phoenix in my youth,
so let them have their day."*

— William Butler Yeats

"It is good to have an end to journey toward,
but it is the journey that matters in the end."
– Japanese proverb signified by the Yatsuhashi,
or eight-fold Japanese bridge.

The University Mace is the symbol of authority of the Chancellor and is displayed on ceremonial occasions, most notably during the annual Congregation ceremonies. In 1957, President Norman MacKenzie asked B.C. Binning, UBC's first head of Fine Arts, to design the object. Binning longed to make the Mace unique, and to that end he commissioned Vancouver carver George Norris to design and carve it. No other Canadian university possesses anything like the UBC Mace. Norris carved it from a block of yew and included a stylized thunderbird on the thick upper portion. The added use of copper helped reflect the Northwest Coast native art tradition from which UBC's Mace is proudly drawn. It was first used at the congregation in October of 1959 when Director of Ceremonies Malcolm McGregor carried it for the first time.

Proud student and proud parent on a day when the sun always seems to shine—even when it rains.

Doctor of Laws (LL.D.), Doctor of Science (D.Sc.) and Doctor of Letters (D.Litt.) are the honorary degrees conferred from time to time by the Senate of the University of British Columbia upon those who have achieved distinction in scholarship or public service. The University first conferred honorary degrees at the inaugural Congregation held at the new Point Grey campus on October 16, 1925.

The list of honorary degree recipients includes:

Allan McEachern, LL.D. Former Chief Justice of the B.C. Court of Appeal. Appointed Chancellor of UBC in 2002. UBC Alumnus.

Louise Arbour, LL.D. Supreme Court Justice and United Nations Security Council prosecutor.

Atom Egoyan, D.Litt. Canadian writer, director, producer and filmmaker.

Peter C. Newman, LL.D. Canadian author, journalist, historian.

Carol Shields, D.Litt. Internationally respected author and novelist, Pulitzer Prize and Governor General's Award recipient.

David Lam, LL.D. Businessman, philanthropist, UBC Alumnus and British Columbia's first Chinese-Canadian Lieutenant Governor.

Beverley McLachlin, LL.D. Chief Justice of the Supreme Court of Canada.

HONORIS CAUSA:
FOR THE SAKE OF HONOUR

Over the years, UBC has presented more than 500 honorary degrees for unparalleled achievement or commitment to public service. (Opposite top) Beverly McLachlin and David Lam. (Above) a young Pat Carney at the typewriter, (left) Kim Campbell and (bottom) John Turner.

Oscar Peterson, LL.D. Internationally admired jazz musician and composer.

Karen Kain, D.LITT. Canada's prima ballerina.

Pierre Elliott Trudeau, LL.D. Prime Minister of Canada 1968 to 1979 and 1980 to 1984; lawyer, scholar, statesman.

Robertson Davies, D.LITT. distinguished novelist, author, journalist and essayist.

Field Marshal Bernard Law Montgomery, LL.D. British Commander of the 8th Army and Commander of the 21st Army Group in World War II.

Senator Pat Carney, LL.D. Award winning journalist, Member of Parliament 1980 to 1988 and Federal Cabinet Minister. UBC Alumna.